THE MIRACLES
OF JESUS
FOR CHILDREN

Edited by
Louis M. Savary

Illustrations by
Rita Goodwill

M_B

THE REGINA PRESS
NEW YORK

THE MIRACLES OF JESUS
FOR
CHILDREN

TABLE OF CONTENTS

JESUS, THE SON OF GOD

About 2,000 years ago, a man lived whose name was Jesus. He was the Son of God.

Wherever he went, crowds came to see him and hear what he had to say.

He told people that God loved them. And to prove it, Jesus would heal people whom nobody else could heal. He could do miracles.

This book tells about some of the ways Jesus' miracles helped people.

WONDERFUL WINE

Jesus and the Apostles were invited to a wedding. His mother Mary was there, too.

Mary noticed that the wine supply was running out and told Jesus. Jesus called the waiters and told them to fill six big waterpots full of water. Then he said, "Dip some out and take it to the head-waiter."

"This is delicious wine," the headwaiter said. And this was the first miracle that Jesus performed.

TOO MANY FISH

Once Jesus got into Peter's boat and told him to go out into the lake to catch some fish.

Peter said, "We've been fishing all night and didn't catch a single fish. But if you say so, we'll try again."

Then as soon as they threw their fishing nets over the side, so many fish swam in that the nets were full and almost broke.

After that miracle, Peter followed Jesus and never left him.

TIME FOR SUPPER

One day, Jesus and his followers were going to Peter's house. Peter had invited everyone for supper. When they arrived at the house, Peter's mother-in-law was sick in bed with a high fever. She was supposed to do the cooking.

So Jesus went over to her and touched her hand. That's all he did, and she got better so fast that she was able to get out of bed and have everything ready in time for supper.

NOT AFRAID OF LEPERS

Suddenly the crowd stopped. "A leper is coming," someone cried.

A leper is somebody with a skin sickness. People were afraid of lepers, so nobody went near them. But Jesus wasn't afraid. He went up to the sick man and asked what he wanted.

"Sir," the leper said, "if you want to, you can heal me."

"I want to," Jesus answered, "Be healed." Instantly all the sickness disappeared. The crowd was amazed.

A PARALYZED BOY

A Roman army officer came to Jesus and said, "A boy who works for me is paralyzed and full of pain. Please come home and heal him."

"Yes," said Jesus. "I will come."

Then the officer said, "Sir, you don't have to come. I know that even right here, if you tell the boy's sickness to go away—it will go."

"Go along home," Jesus said. And when the officer got home, he found the boy cured.

THROUGH THE ROOF

Four men carrying a stretcher arrived outside a crowded house. They brought a friend who was paralyzed. They wanted Jesus to heal him, but there was no way to get in.

So they dug through the clay roof. And when the hole was big enough, they lowered their paralyzed friend by ropes right in front of Jesus.

Jesus healed the sick man. Next day, everybody helped repair the roof they had broken.

STRETCH YOUR ARM

One sabbath in synagogue, Jesus noticed a man with a deformed arm. He was ashamed of it and kept it hidden.

Some people would be angry at Jesus if he did a miracle now, because that would be doing work on the sabbath, which wasn't allowed.

But Jesus said that helping people is more important, so he told the sick man, "Stretch out your arm."

When the man stretched out his arm, it became normal just like the other one.

ONLY SLEEPING

"My little daughter has just died," a rabbi cried to Jesus, "but you can bring her back to life again."

When Jesus arrived at the rabbi's home, people were weeping loudly as the funeral music was played.

Jesus said, "Please ask everyone to leave. The little girl isn't dead, she's only sleeping."

People sneered at him. "We know when somebody is dead," they said.

Then Jesus took the girl by the hand and she awoke and was alive again.

SUDDENLY THEY COULD SEE

One day, two blind men followed Jesus, holding each other's hands and using their sticks to find the way.

Jesus asked them, "Do you believe that I can make you see?"

"Yes, we do," they told him.

Then he touched their eyes and said, "Because you believe, it will happen."

And suddenly they could see. They looked at one another and laughed and hugged. Their joy knew no bounds.

ALL ALONE IN THE WORLD

A funeral procession carried a young boy who had died. At the village gate, Jesus saw the boy's mother. She was walking next to the coffin and crying. She was a widow and had no other living relative. She was all alone in the world.

Jesus told her, "Don't cry." Then he walked over to the coffin and said, "Young man, come back to life again."

And the boy sat up and began to talk. And Jesus gave him back to his mother.

TO TOUCH HIS COAT

Jesus was walking along, the crowds all around him. A woman who wanted to be healed came beside him and touched his coat.

She had been sick for twelve years and could find no cure. She had tried every doctor in town and had spent all her money on medicines they told her to take. But the instant she touched Jesus' coat, her sickness stopped.

Jesus blessed her. "Go in peace," he said.

FOOD FOR EVERYONE

One day Jesus was teaching in the countryside.

At night, the crowd was still there, and they had nothing to eat. There were over 5,000 people. One boy had five loaves of bread and two fishes. Jesus blessed the loaves and fishes and gave them to his followers and said, "Feed everybody."

Then the food kept multiplying until there was enough for all. And there were lots of leftovers, too.

A TERRIBLE STORM

Jesus said to his friends, "Let's go in our boat and cross the lake." That day Jesus was so tired, he fell asleep in the back of the boat.

Next came a heavy rainstorm. The Apostles were afraid the boat would sink and they would all drown. "Help!" they shouted to Jesus.

Then Jesus spoke to the wind and the sea. "Quiet down," he said. And the wind stopped, and the sea became calm.

A WILD MAN

A wild man lived in a cemetery like an animal. People chained him, but he would break the chains as if they were pieces of string. Nothing was strong enough to control him.

When this man came up to Jesus, he fell down in front of him. He was afraid of Jesus.

"Come out of this man, you evil spirits," said Jesus, talking to the demons who lived inside the wild man, tormenting him. And the wild man then became a normal, human being.

NOW I CAN SEE

People brought a blind man to Jesus. First, he wet the man's eyes and then laid his hands over them. "Can you see anything now?" Jesus asked.

The man looked around, "Yes," he said, "I can see people over there, but not very clearly. They look like tree trunks walking around."

So Jesus put his hands over the blind man's eyes again until his eyes were perfect. "I can see everything well now," said the blind man. "How can I ever thank you?"